CoPilot Unleashed:

A Comprehensive Guide to
Mastering this Powerful AI Assistant

Terry C. Power

Table of Contents

Introduction

In an era defined by rapid technological evolution, the
landscape of digital interaction is undergoing a profound

transformation. We've moved beyond the era of point-and-click, transitioning towards a future where our relationship with technology is more intuitive, more conversational, and, frankly, more human.

Imagine a world where your digital tools understand your intent, anticipate your needs, and seamlessly integrate into your daily workflow. Picture an assistant that not only responds to your commands but also learns from your habits, adapting to your unique preferences. This isn't science fiction; it's the promise of CoPilot.

You know that feeling when you're wrestling with a complex task, searching for a specific function buried deep within a menu, or trying to decipher cryptic error messages? It's a universal frustration, a digital bottleneck that slows us down and saps our productivity. But what if there was a better way? What if you could simply ask your computer to perform the task, in plain, natural language?

That's precisely what Microsoft's CoPilot aims to achieve. It's not just another AI chatbot; it's a paradigm shift, a reimagining of how we interact with our digital environment. CoPilot is designed to be your intelligent partner, a conversational AI that's deeply integrated into the tools you use every day, from your operating system to your productivity apps.

This book, "CoPilot Unleashed: Your Conversational AI Powerhouse," is your comprehensive guide to understanding and mastering this revolutionary technology. We'll explore the core concepts behind CoPilot, delve into its diverse applications, and reveal the secrets to unlocking its full potential.

We'll journey through the intricacies of CoPilot's integration with Microsoft's ecosystem, from seamless interactions within Edge and Bing to the power of the dedicated desktop application. We'll discover how CoPilot transforms everyday tasks, from drafting documents and creating presentations to conducting in-depth research and generating creative content.

But we won't just scratch the surface. We'll dive deep into the advanced capabilities of CoPilot, comparing its "Deep Thinking" features to other leading AI models like ChatGPT, Gemini, and Perplexity. We'll explore the power of multimodal interaction, from drawing images to engaging in audible searches.

Throughout this book, you'll find real-life examples and practical use cases that illustrate the transformative power of CoPilot. Whether you're a seasoned tech enthusiast or a curious beginner, you'll gain valuable insights into how CoPilot can enhance your productivity, creativity, and overall digital experience.

So, buckle up and get ready to embark on a journey into the world of conversational AI. "CoPilot Unleashed" is your key to unlocking the power of this groundbreaking technology, empowering you to navigate the future of digital interaction with confidence and ease. Let's begin.

Chapter 1: CoPilot Vision

Alright, let's talk about vision. Not the kind where you see into the future, although, with AI, sometimes it feels that way! We're talking about CoPilot's "vision" in the sense of its overarching purpose, its design philosophy, and where Microsoft is aiming to take this powerful tool.

Think of CoPilot as your intelligent assistant, woven into the fabric of your digital life. It's not just a chatbot; it's a contextual, adaptive, and increasingly multimodal companion. You know, like having a super-smart friend who's always there to help, but lives inside your computer and phone.

So, what's the big idea? Microsoft envisions CoPilot as a universal interface, a way to interact with technology more naturally and efficiently. You know how sometimes you fumble through menus or get lost in a sea of options? CoPilot aims to cut through the clutter. Imagine, instead of searching for a specific setting, you simply say, "Adjust the screen brightness to 75%," and it's done. That's the vision.

Now, let's get a bit technical, but not too scary. CoPilot is built on large language models (LLMs), which are trained on massive amounts of text and code. These LLMs enable CoPilot to understand natural language, generate text, and even write code. But it's more than just an LLM. Microsoft has integrated CoPilot deeply into its ecosystem, connecting it to its productivity apps, its operating system, and its search engine.

Let's take a practical example. Imagine you're working on a presentation in PowerPoint. You need to create a slide summarizing your company's quarterly sales data. Instead of manually entering the data and creating a chart, you can simply ask CoPilot, "Create a slide summarizing the quarterly sales data from this Excel file." CoPilot will then analyze the Excel file, generate the slide, and even suggest a suitable chart. That's the power of integration.

But here's where things get interesting: CoPilot is designed to be personalized and adaptive. It learns from your usage patterns and preferences, tailoring its responses and suggestions to your specific needs. It's not a one-size-fits-all solution. For example, if you frequently use a particular set of tools or commands, CoPilot will prioritize those options, making them readily accessible.

Let's talk about the user experience. Microsoft is focusing on making CoPilot as seamless and intuitive as possible. You know how frustrating it is when a technology feels clunky or awkward? CoPilot aims to avoid that. The goal is to make it feel like a natural extension of your workflow, a tool that enhances your productivity without getting in your way.

Here's a real-life scenario: A marketing team is brainstorming ideas for a new campaign. They're using Microsoft Teams to collaborate, and they're struggling to come up with fresh ideas. One team member suggests using CoPilot to generate some creative concepts. They ask CoPilot, "Generate five creative campaign ideas for a new sustainable product launch targeting Gen Z." Within seconds, CoPilot provides a list of innovative and engaging ideas, sparking a productive discussion.

Now, let's address a common concern: privacy. Microsoft recognizes the importance of data security and privacy. CoPilot is designed with robust security measures in place to protect your data. Microsoft also provides users with control over their data, allowing them to manage their privacy settings and opt out of certain features.

Okay, so we've covered the vision, the technology, and the user experience. But what about the future? Where is CoPilot headed? Microsoft is continuously developing and enhancing CoPilot, adding new features and capabilities. One area of focus is multimodal interaction, which means CoPilot will be able to understand and respond to various forms of input, including voice, images, and video.

Imagine, for example, being able to show CoPilot a picture of a product and ask it to find similar products online. Or being able to use voice commands to control your computer, even in noisy environments. That's the future of CoPilot.

Another area of development is deep integration with third-party apps and services. This will allow CoPilot to extend its capabilities beyond the Microsoft ecosystem, becoming a truly universal assistant.

Let's think about this in a real world application. A construction manager uses a 3D model of a building in progress. He wants to know if a specific pipe route is compliant with local building codes. He uploads the model to a CoPilot integrated application, and asks "Is this pipe route up to code?". Copilot then analyses the 3d model, and compares the pipe route to the local building codes, and provides a clear response, and highlights any areas that are not compliant.

In conclusion, CoPilot's vision is to transform the way we interact with technology, making it more natural, efficient, and personalized. It's not just a tool; it's a companion, a partner, and a powerful ally in our digital lives. And with continuous development and innovation, CoPilot's potential is limitless.

Chapter 2: CoPilot and Word

Okay, so you've got this powerful AI assistant, CoPilot, and you're working on a document. Maybe it's a report, a proposal, or even just a simple letter. How do you actually make CoPilot work *for* you within the context of document creation? That's what we're going to unpack in this chapter.

Imagine you're staring at a blank page. We've all been there. That blinking cursor, the mental block. It's a universal struggle. But now, instead of facing that blank page alone, you have CoPilot.

Let's start with the basics. CoPilot is integrated directly into Microsoft Word. This means it understands the context of your document, the content you've already written, and even your writing style. It's not just a generic chatbot spitting out text; it's a contextual assistant that adapts to your specific needs.

You know how sometimes you struggle to find the right words? Or maybe you're stuck on a particular section and need a fresh perspective? CoPilot can help with that. You can simply ask it to "summarize this paragraph," "rewrite this sentence in a more professional tone," or even "generate a list of bullet points based on this section."

Let's take a practical example. You're writing a report on climate change, and you're struggling to explain a complex scientific concept. You can highlight the relevant section and ask CoPilot, "Explain this concept in simpler terms for a non-technical audience." CoPilot will then rewrite the section, breaking down the complex jargon into clear, concise language.

Or, let's say you're writing a proposal, and you need to include some supporting data. You can ask CoPilot to "find relevant statistics on [topic]" and it will search the web and provide you with relevant information. You can then easily insert that information into your document, with proper citations, of course.

But CoPilot isn't just about rewriting and summarizing. It can also help you generate new content. Imagine you need to write an introduction for your report, but you're not sure where to start. You can simply ask CoPilot, "Write an introduction for a report on [topic]," and it will generate a draft that you can then edit and refine.

Here's where things get interesting: CoPilot can also help you with formatting and styling. You know how tedious it can be to manually format a long document? CoPilot can automate that process. You can ask it to "apply heading styles to this section," "create a table of contents," or even "format this document according to APA style."

Let's think about a real-world scenario. A student is writing a research paper. They've gathered a lot of information, but they're struggling to organize it into a coherent argument. They use CoPilot to generate an outline, which helps them structure their paper and ensure that their arguments flow logically. They then use CoPilot to refine their writing, ensuring that their paper is clear, concise, and well-supported.

Now, let's talk about collaboration. You know how sometimes you need to work on a document with multiple people, and it can be a nightmare to keep track of changes and comments? CoPilot can streamline the collaboration process. You can use it to suggest edits, provide feedback, and even track changes in real time.

For example, a team is working on a marketing plan. They use CoPilot to generate a draft of the plan, and then they collaborate on the document, using CoPilot to suggest edits and provide feedback. CoPilot also helps them track changes and ensure that everyone is on the same page.

Here's another practical example. A lawyer is drafting a contract. They use CoPilot to generate a first draft, and then they use it to check for legal errors and inconsistencies. CoPilot can even suggest alternative clauses and provide legal citations.

Let's address a common concern: plagiarism. With CoPilot, it's crucial to understand that it's a tool, not a replacement for your own critical thinking and creativity. You should always review and edit the content generated by CoPilot, ensuring that it accurately reflects your own ideas and that you provide proper citations for any external sources.

Here's a tip: use CoPilot as a brainstorming partner. If you're stuck on a particular section, ask CoPilot to generate a few different versions, and then use those versions as a starting point for your own writing.

You could ask, "Give me three different ways to phrase this sentence, each with a different tone." This allows for a more creative process.

Remember, CoPilot is designed to enhance your writing, not replace it. It's a powerful tool that can help you write faster, more efficiently, and more effectively. But ultimately, the quality of your writing depends on your own skills and judgment.

In conclusion, CoPilot is a game-changer for document creation. It can help you with everything from generating content and formatting documents to collaborating with others and ensuring accuracy. By understanding how to use CoPilot effectively, you can unlock its full potential and transform the way you write.

Chapter 3: Using CoPilot with Edge

Okay, so we've talked about CoPilot in general, and how it can help with document creation. Now, let's zoom in on a specific application: Microsoft Edge. You know, that web browser you might use to surf the internet, read articles, watch videos, and all that good stuff? Well, CoPilot is deeply integrated into Edge, and it can significantly enhance your browsing experience.

Think of Edge as your digital gateway to the world of information. And CoPilot is your intelligent guide, helping you navigate that world more efficiently and effectively. It's not just about searching for information; it's about understanding it, summarizing it, and using it in meaningful ways.

Let's start with the basics. CoPilot in Edge can help you with your everyday browsing tasks. You know how sometimes you have a question and you need to quickly find the answer? You can simply ask CoPilot in the sidebar, and it will search the web and provide you with relevant information.

For example, you're planning a trip to Paris, and you want to know the best time to visit. You can ask CoPilot, "What is the best time to visit Paris?" and it will provide you with information about the weather, tourist crowds, and events.

But CoPilot in Edge goes beyond simple search. It can also help you understand and summarize web pages. You know how sometimes you come across a long article or a dense research paper, and you don't have time to read the whole thing? CoPilot can help you get the gist of it quickly.

Here's how it works: you can simply ask CoPilot to "summarize this page," and it will analyze the content and provide you with a concise summary. This can be incredibly useful for quickly getting up to speed on a topic or for identifying the key takeaways from a lengthy document.

Let's take a practical example. You're researching a new technology, and you come across a detailed technical report. You don't have time to read the entire report, so you ask CoPilot to summarize it. CoPilot provides you with a concise summary of the key findings, allowing you to quickly understand the main points.

Now, let's talk about creativity. CoPilot in Edge can also help you generate creative content. You know how sometimes you need to write an email, a social media post, or even a poem, and you're struggling to find the right words? CoPilot can help you get started.

You can ask it to "write an email to [person] about [topic]," or "generate a social media post about [topic]," and it will provide you with a draft that you can then edit and refine.

Here's where things get interesting: CoPilot in Edge can also help you with shopping. You know how sometimes you're looking for a specific product, and you're struggling to find the best deal? CoPilot can help you compare prices, read reviews, and find the best options.

For example, you're looking for a new laptop. You can ask CoPilot to "find the best deals on laptops with these specifications," and it will search the web and provide you with a list of options, along with prices and reviews.

Let's think about a real-world scenario. A student is researching for a project. They're using Edge to browse different websites, and they're using CoPilot to summarize articles, find relevant information, and generate citations. CoPilot helps them save time and stay organized, allowing them to focus on their research.

Now, let's talk about accessibility. CoPilot in Edge can also help make the web more accessible to everyone. You know how sometimes websites can be difficult to navigate, especially for people with disabilities? CoPilot can help by providing alternative ways to interact with web pages.

For example, it can read aloud the content of a web page, or it can provide alternative descriptions for images.

Here's another practical example. A user with a visual impairment is browsing the web. They're using CoPilot to read aloud the content of web pages, and they're using it to navigate websites using voice commands. CoPilot helps them access information and interact with the web more easily.

Let's address a common concern: privacy. Microsoft understands the importance of privacy, and CoPilot in Edge is designed with privacy in mind. You have control over your data, and you can adjust your privacy settings to suit your preferences.

Here's a tip: use CoPilot in Edge to translate web pages. If you come across a website in a language you don't understand, you can ask CoPilot to translate it for you. This can be incredibly useful for accessing information from around the world.

You could say, "Translate this page into Spanish," or "Summarize this page in French."

Remember, CoPilot in Edge is designed to enhance your browsing experience, making it more efficient, informative, and enjoyable. It's a powerful tool that can help you get the most out of the web.

In conclusion, CoPilot in Edge is a versatile tool that can help you with a wide range of tasks, from searching for information and summarizing web pages to generating creative content and shopping. By understanding how to use CoPilot effectively, you can unlock its full potential and transform the way you browse the web.

Chapter 4: The CoPilot Desktop Application

Alright, we've explored how CoPilot integrates with specific applications like Word and Edge. Now, let's zoom out and talk about CoPilot as a standalone application on your desktop. Think of it as CoPilot in its purest form, a dedicated space where you can interact with the AI assistant directly, unconstrained by the context of a specific program.

Imagine having a central hub for all your CoPilot interactions. That's essentially what the CoPilot desktop application provides. It's like having a universal window to your AI assistant, allowing you to ask questions, generate content, and perform tasks without needing to switch between different applications.

Let's start with the core functionality. The CoPilot desktop application serves as a powerful conversational interface. You can type or speak your requests, and CoPilot will respond accordingly. It's like having a direct line to an intelligent assistant that's always ready to help.

For example, you can ask CoPilot to "write a summary of the latest news," "generate a list of ideas for a birthday gift," or "calculate the tip for a restaurant bill." CoPilot will process your request and provide you with a relevant and informative response.

But the CoPilot desktop application is more than just a chat interface. It also provides access to a range of features and capabilities. Think of it as a central command center for your AI assistant.

Here's where things get interesting: The CoPilot desktop application can also integrate with other applications on your computer. This allows you to perform tasks that span across different programs.

For example, you could ask CoPilot to "open a specific file," "send an email," or "schedule a meeting" directly from the desktop application. CoPilot will then interact with the relevant applications to carry out your request.

Let's take a practical example. You're working on a project that involves multiple files and applications. You can use the CoPilot desktop application to manage your workflow, asking it to open specific files, switch between applications, and even automate repetitive tasks. This can significantly streamline your work process and boost your productivity.

Think about a real-world scenario. A project manager is using the CoPilot desktop application to manage a team's tasks. They use it to assign tasks, track progress, and communicate with team members. CoPilot helps them stay organized and ensure that the project stays on track.

Now, let's talk about customization. The CoPilot desktop application can often be customized to suit your preferences. You might be able to adjust the appearance, configure settings, and even add custom commands.

For example, you could customize the appearance of the CoPilot desktop application to match your desktop theme, or you could add custom commands to automate specific tasks.

Here's another practical example. A user is using the CoPilot desktop application to control their smart home devices. They have added custom commands to turn on the lights, adjust the thermostat, and lock the doors. CoPilot becomes their central hub for controlling their home environment.

Let's address a common question: How is the CoPilot desktop application different from using CoPilot within a specific application like Word or Edge?

The key difference lies in the context. When you use CoPilot within a specific application, it's typically focused on tasks related to that application. For example, in Word, CoPilot is primarily focused on document creation and editing.

In contrast, the CoPilot desktop application provides a more general-purpose interface, allowing you to interact with CoPilot across different applications and perform a wider range of tasks.

Here's a tip: Use the CoPilot desktop application for tasks that require you to interact with multiple applications or for tasks that don't fall neatly within the context of a specific application.

For example, if you need to gather information from multiple sources, summarize that information, and then create a presentation, you could use the CoPilot desktop application to manage the entire workflow.

Remember, the CoPilot desktop application is designed to provide you with a central and convenient way to interact with your AI assistant. It's a powerful tool that can help you streamline your workflow, boost your productivity, and get things done more efficiently.

In conclusion, the CoPilot desktop application offers a versatile and powerful way to interact with CoPilot. It provides a central hub for your AI interactions, allowing you to ask questions, generate content, and perform tasks across different applications. By understanding how to use the CoPilot desktop application effectively, you can unlock its full potential and transform the way you work and interact with your computer.

Chapter 5: Interact with CoPilot via Voice

In the evolving landscape of human-computer interaction, the ability to communicate with technology using our voice is rapidly becoming a cornerstone of the user experience. CoPilot, at the forefront of this trend, offers robust capabilities for audible interaction, transforming how we engage with our digital world. This chapter explores the nuances of interacting with CoPilot audibly, covering everything from basic voice commands to advanced conversational scenarios, and the implications for accessibility and productivity.

Imagine a world where you're no longer tethered to a keyboard or mouse. Your voice becomes the primary interface, allowing you to seamlessly interact with

CoPilot, whether you're multitasking, on the go, or simply seeking a more natural and intuitive way to communicate with your digital assistant. This is the promise of audible interaction with CoPilot.

The Power of Natural Language Processing

At the heart of CoPilot's ability to understand and respond to voice commands lies Natural Language Processing (NLP). NLP is a branch of Artificial Intelligence that focuses on enabling computers to understand, interpret, and generate human language. It's the engine that powers CoPilot's capacity to decipher the complexities of spoken language, including variations in accent, intonation, and vocabulary.

CoPilot's NLP capabilities are constantly being refined, allowing it to handle increasingly complex and nuanced requests. This means you can interact with CoPilot using natural, conversational language, rather than needing to memorize rigid commands. You can say things like, "Hey CoPilot, remind me to pick up groceries on my way home," or "CoPilot, summarize the key points of this document," and CoPilot will understand your intent and take appropriate action.

Setting Up for Audible Interaction

Before you can start using your voice to interact with CoPilot, you'll need to ensure that your device is properly configured. This typically involves:

- **Enabling the Microphone:** Most devices have built-in microphones, but you may need to enable them in your device's settings.

- **Activating Voice Activation:** CoPilot may have a specific activation phrase, such as "Hey CoPilot," that you need to enable. This allows CoPilot to listen for your commands.

- **Adjusting Settings:** You may also be able to adjust settings related to voice input, such as language preferences or noise cancellation.

The specific steps for setting up audible interaction may vary depending on your device and operating system, but the general process is usually straightforward.

Basic Voice Commands and Use Cases

Once you've set up your device for voice input, you can start using CoPilot for a wide range of tasks. Here are some basic voice commands and use cases:

- **Launching Applications:** You can use voice commands to quickly open applications. For example, you can say, "Open Microsoft Word," or "Launch Google Chrome." This is particularly useful for hands-free operation or when you need to switch between applications quickly.

- Navigating the Web: CoPilot can help you navigate the web using voice commands. You can say things like, "Go to Google.com," or "Search for the best restaurants near me." This can be a convenient way to browse the web without having to use a keyboard or mouse.

- Controlling Media: CoPilot can also be used to control media playback. You can say, "Play music," "Pause the video," or "Skip to the next song." This is useful for controlling media while you're multitasking or when your hands are occupied.

- Setting Reminders and Alarms: Voice commands are an excellent way to set reminders and alarms. You can say, "Set an alarm for 7:00 AM," or "Remind me to call my doctor tomorrow." This is a quick and easy way to stay organized and manage your time.

- Sending Messages and Emails: CoPilot can help you send messages and emails using voice commands. You can say, "Send a message to John saying I'll be late," or "Email Sarah to confirm the meeting." This can be a convenient way to communicate without having to type.

These are just a few examples of the many ways you can use basic voice commands with CoPilot. As you become more familiar with CoPilot's capabilities, you'll discover even more ways to use your voice to interact with your digital assistant.

Advanced Conversational Scenarios

Beyond basic commands, CoPilot excels at handling more complex and conversational scenarios. This is where the true power of NLP comes into play. You can engage in natural dialogues with CoPilot, asking follow-up questions, providing context, and refining your requests.

Here are some examples of advanced conversational scenarios:

- Complex Information Retrieval: You can ask CoPilot complex questions that require it to gather information from multiple sources. For example, you can say, "CoPilot, compare the features of these three laptops and tell me which one is the best value for money." CoPilot will then analyze the information and provide you with a detailed comparison.

- Task Automation: CoPilot can help you automate complex tasks using voice commands. For example, you can say, "CoPilot, book a flight to

New York for next Friday, find a hotel near Times Square, and add it to my calendar." CoPilot will then handle all the necessary steps to complete the task.

- **Creative Content Generation:** CoPilot can even help you generate creative content using voice commands. You can say, "CoPilot, write a short story about a robot who falls in love," or "CoPilot, compose a poem about the beauty of nature." CoPilot will then use its language generation capabilities to create the content.

- **Personalized Assistance:** CoPilot can learn from your preferences and habits, providing personalized assistance based on your individual needs. For example, you can say, "CoPilot, tell me about my schedule for today," or "CoPilot, recommend some restaurants based on my past preferences." CoPilot will then provide you with personalized information and recommendations.

These advanced scenarios demonstrate the potential of CoPilot to become a truly intelligent and helpful companion, capable of understanding and responding to a wide range of complex and nuanced requests.

Accessibility and Inclusivity

Audible interaction with CoPilot has significant implications for accessibility and inclusivity. It can provide a more accessible way for people with disabilities to interact with technology, allowing them to control their devices and access information using their voice.

For example, people with mobility impairments can use voice commands to control their computers and devices, without having to rely on a keyboard or mouse. People with visual impairments can use voice commands to navigate the web and access information, without having to rely on screen readers.

CoPilot's audible interaction capabilities can help to create a more inclusive digital environment, where everyone can participate and benefit from technology.

Tips for Effective Audible Interaction

To get the most out of audible interaction with CoPilot, here are some tips:

- **Speak Clearly and Naturally**: Speak clearly and at a normal pace. Avoid using overly formal or technical language.

- **Minimize Background Noise**: Try to minimize background noise to ensure that CoPilot can accurately understand your commands.

- **Use Natural Language:** Use natural, conversational language. Avoid using rigid commands or keywords.

- **Provide Context:** Provide context when necessary. For example, if you're asking CoPilot to send a message, specify the recipient and the message content.

- **Be Patient:** CoPilot is constantly learning and improving, but it may not always understand your commands perfectly. Be patient and try rephrasing your request if necessary.

By following these tips, you can improve the accuracy and effectiveness of your audible interactions with CoPilot.

The Future of Audible Interaction

The future of audible interaction with CoPilot is bright. As NLP technology continues to advance, CoPilot will become even better at understanding and responding to human language. We can expect to see even more sophisticated conversational scenarios, more personalized assistance, and even greater accessibility.

Imagine a future where you can have truly natural and seamless conversations with CoPilot, where it can anticipate your needs, understand your emotions, and provide proactive assistance. This is the vision of the future of audible interaction, and CoPilot is leading the way.

In conclusion, interacting with CoPilot audibly is a powerful and transformative way to engage with technology. It offers a more natural, intuitive, and accessible way to control your devices, access information, and perform tasks. As CoPilot's NLP capabilities continue to evolve, the potential for audible interaction is limitless, paving the way for a future where our voices become the primary interface to our digital world.

Chapter 6: CoPilot on a Mobile Application

In today's fast-paced world, our smartphones have become indispensable tools, serving as our primary means of communication, information access, and productivity. Recognizing this, Microsoft has brought CoPilot to mobile devices, extending its capabilities beyond desktops and laptops. This chapter delves into the intricacies of using CoPilot on a mobile application, exploring its features, benefits, and how it transforms the mobile experience.

Imagine having the power of CoPilot in your pocket, accessible anytime, anywhere. That's the reality with CoPilot on a mobile application. It's about bringing the intelligence and assistance of CoPilot to the device you use most often, making your mobile experience more efficient, productive, and enjoyable.

The Mobile Revolution and AI Integration

The mobile revolution has transformed how we interact with technology. Smartphones have become powerful computing devices, capable of handling a wide range of tasks. This has paved the way for the integration of AI assistants like CoPilot into mobile applications.

By embedding CoPilot into a mobile app, Microsoft is capitalizing on the ubiquity of smartphones and the growing demand for mobile productivity. It's about meeting users where they are, providing them with a seamless and intuitive way to access the benefits of AI assistance while on the go.

Key Features of CoPilot on Mobile

CoPilot on a mobile application offers a range of features designed to enhance the mobile experience. These features may vary slightly depending on the specific app and platform, but some common key features include:

- Voice Interaction: Like its desktop counterpart, CoPilot on mobile supports voice commands, allowing for hands-free interaction. This is particularly useful for tasks like setting reminders, making calls, or getting directions while driving.

- Text-Based Chat: Users can also interact with CoPilot through text-based chat, providing a familiar and convenient way to ask questions, give commands, and receive information.

- Contextual Awareness: CoPilot on mobile is designed to be contextually aware, meaning it can understand the context of your current activity and provide relevant assistance. For example, if you're viewing a website in your mobile browser, CoPilot can help you summarize the content or find related information.

- Integration with Mobile Apps: CoPilot can integrate with other mobile apps, allowing for seamless workflows. For example, it might be able to help you draft an email in your email app or create a calendar event in your calendar app.

- Personalized Assistance: CoPilot on mobile can learn from your usage patterns and preferences, providing personalized assistance tailored to your individual needs.

Benefits of Using CoPilot on Mobile

Using CoPilot on a mobile application offers a range of benefits, including:

- Increased Productivity: CoPilot can help you get more done on the go, by automating tasks, providing quick access to information, and streamlining workflows.

- Enhanced Efficiency: CoPilot can help you save time and effort by providing relevant information and assistance when you need it, without having to search through multiple apps or websites.

- Improved Accessibility: CoPilot on mobile can make technology more accessible to people with disabilities, by providing alternative ways to interact with their devices, such as voice commands.

- Seamless Integration: CoPilot's integration with other mobile apps creates a seamless and intuitive user experience, allowing you to perform tasks across different apps without having to switch between them.

- Personalized Experience: CoPilot's ability to learn from your preferences and habits ensures that you receive relevant and personalized assistance, making your mobile experience more efficient and enjoyable.

Use Cases for CoPilot on Mobile

CoPilot on mobile can be used in a variety of situations, including:

- **On-the-Go Productivity:** CoPilot can help you stay productive while you're on the go, by allowing you to manage your schedule, create to-do lists, draft emails, and access important information.

- **Travel Assistance:** CoPilot can be a valuable travel companion, providing real-time information about flights, hotels, and local attractions, as well as helping you navigate unfamiliar cities.

- **Information Access:** CoPilot can provide quick and easy access to information, allowing you to search the web, get answers to your questions, and stay up-to-date on the latest news.

- **Communication:** CoPilot can help you communicate more effectively, by helping you draft messages, translate languages, and stay connected with your contacts.

- **Entertainment:** CoPilot can enhance your entertainment experience, by helping you find new music, movies, and TV shows, as well as providing information about your favorite artists and actors.

Real-World Examples

Here are some real-world examples of how CoPilot can be used on a mobile application:

- A business professional uses CoPilot to manage their schedule, draft emails, and prepare for meetings while commuting to work.

- A student uses CoPilot to research for a project, take notes in class, and create study guides.

- A traveler uses CoPilot to get directions, find restaurants, and translate languages while visiting a foreign country.

- A person with a disability uses CoPilot to control their device, access information, and communicate with others using voice commands.

Challenges and Considerations

While CoPilot on mobile offers many benefits, there are also some challenges and considerations to keep in mind:

- Battery Life: Using AI assistants on mobile devices can consume battery power, so it's important to be mindful of your device's battery life.

- **Privacy:** It's important to be aware of the privacy implications of using AI assistants on mobile devices, as they may collect and store your data.

- **Accuracy:** While CoPilot's accuracy is constantly improving, it may not always understand your requests perfectly, especially in noisy environments or when using voice commands.

- **Connectivity:** CoPilot requires an internet connection to function, so it may not be available in areas with limited or no connectivity.

The Future of CoPilot on Mobile

The future of CoPilot on mobile is promising, with continued advancements in AI and mobile technology. We can expect to see even more sophisticated features and capabilities, as well as deeper integration with other mobile apps and services.

Imagine a future where CoPilot becomes an even more integral part of our mobile lives, seamlessly anticipating our needs, providing proactive assistance, and transforming the way we interact with our smartphones.

In conclusion, CoPilot on a mobile application brings the power of AI assistance to the palm of your hand, enhancing productivity, efficiency, and accessibility. By understanding its features, benefits, and considerations, you can unlock its full potential and transform your mobile experience.

Chapter 7: CoPilot Deep Thinking Application

In the realm of Artificial Intelligence, the ability to perform complex reasoning and problem-solving is a hallmark of advanced capabilities. CoPilot, in its evolution, has ventured into this territory with its "Deep Thinking" application. This chapter explores the nuances of CoPilot's Deep Thinking application, examining its core functionalities, how it differs from standard AI interactions, and its potential impact across various fields.

Imagine CoPilot moving beyond simple responses to complex analysis, tackling intricate problems, and providing insights that were previously out of reach. That's the essence of the Deep Thinking application – it's CoPilot stepping into the domain of advanced AI reasoning.

The Evolution of AI and Deep Thinking

To understand CoPilot's Deep Thinking application, it's crucial to appreciate the evolution of AI. Early AI systems were often rule-based, following predefined instructions. Modern AI, particularly with the advent of deep learning, has moved towards learning from vast amounts of data, enabling it to recognize patterns, make predictions, and generate human-like text.

However, "Deep Thinking" represents a further leap. It's about AI not just processing information, but truly understanding it, making connections, and engaging in abstract reasoning. It's about moving beyond pattern recognition to cognitive simulation.

CoPilot's Deep Thinking application embodies this evolution, aiming to provide users with a tool that can assist with complex tasks that require more than just quick answers or simple text generation.

Core Functionalities of CoPilot Deep Thinking

CoPilot's Deep Thinking application is designed with several core functionalities that set it apart:

- Complex Problem Solving: Unlike standard AI interactions that might involve answering a specific question, Deep Thinking is geared towards tackling complex problems that require multiple steps, analysis of various factors, and creative solutions.

- Advanced Reasoning: Deep Thinking enables CoPilot to engage in more sophisticated reasoning, including deductive reasoning (drawing conclusions from given information), inductive reasoning (forming generalizations from specific examples), and abductive reasoning (making the best possible explanation given incomplete information).

- **In-Depth Analysis:** The application is designed to analyze large and complex datasets, identify trends and patterns, and provide insights that might not be immediately apparent.

- **Contextual Understanding:** Deep Thinking enhances CoPilot's ability to understand context, allowing it to grasp the subtleties of a situation, consider different perspectives, and provide more nuanced responses.

- **Hypothesis Generation:** CoPilot Deep Thinking can generate hypotheses, explore different scenarios, and evaluate potential outcomes, assisting users in strategic planning and decision-making.

How CoPilot Deep Thinking Differs from Standard AI

CoPilot's Deep Thinking application is distinct from standard AI interactions in several key ways:

- **Depth of Analysis:** Standard AI might provide a quick answer or generate a short text, while Deep

Thinking involves a more thorough and in-depth analysis of the subject matter.

- **Complexity of Tasks:** Deep Thinking is designed for complex tasks that require more than just information retrieval or simple text generation. It's about assisting with problem-solving, decision-making, and strategic planning.

- **Cognitive Simulation:** Deep Thinking aims to simulate more advanced cognitive processes, such as reasoning, analysis, and hypothesis generation, going beyond pattern recognition and simple responses.

- **User Interaction:** Interactions with Deep Thinking might be more iterative, involving a back-and-forth dialogue where the user provides feedback and CoPilot refines its analysis or solutions.

Potential Applications of CoPilot Deep Thinking

The potential applications of CoPilot's Deep Thinking application are vast and span across various fields:

- **Research and Development:** Deep Thinking can assist researchers in analyzing complex datasets, generating hypotheses, and accelerating the pace of discovery.

- **Business Strategy:** Deep Thinking can help businesses with strategic planning, market analysis, risk assessment, and decision-making.

- **Financial Analysis:** Deep Thinking can be used to analyze financial data, identify investment opportunities, and manage risk.

- **Legal Analysis:** Deep Thinking can assist lawyers in analyzing legal documents, conducting research, and developing legal strategies.

- **Scientific Modeling:** Deep Thinking can be used to create and analyze complex scientific models, helping scientists understand and predict natural phenomena.

Examples of CoPilot Deep Thinking in Action

Here are some examples of how CoPilot's Deep Thinking application might be used:

- **A scientist uses Deep Thinking to analyze a large genomic dataset, identify potential drug targets, and develop new therapies.**

- **A business analyst uses Deep Thinking to analyze market trends, identify competitive advantages, and develop a new marketing strategy.**

- A financial analyst uses Deep Thinking to analyze financial data, identify investment risks, and develop a portfolio management strategy.

- A lawyer uses Deep Thinking to analyze legal documents, identify relevant case law, and develop a legal argument.

- An engineer uses Deep Thinking to design and optimize complex systems, such as transportation networks or energy grids.

Challenges and Considerations

While CoPilot's Deep Thinking application holds immense potential, there are also challenges and considerations:

- **Accuracy and Reliability:** Deep Thinking involves complex reasoning, and it's crucial to ensure the accuracy and reliability of the AI's analysis and conclusions.

- **Bias and Fairness:** AI systems can be susceptible to bias, and it's important to address potential biases in Deep Thinking applications to ensure fairness and equity.

- **Transparency and Explainability:** It's important to understand how Deep Thinking arrives at its conclusions, requiring transparency and explainability in the AI's reasoning process.

- Ethical Implications: Deep Thinking applications raise ethical considerations, such as the potential impact on employment, decision-making autonomy, and the responsible use of AI.

The Future of CoPilot Deep Thinking

The future of CoPilot's Deep Thinking application is filled with potential. As AI technology continues to advance, we can expect to see even more sophisticated capabilities, greater accuracy, and wider adoption across various fields.

Imagine a future where Deep Thinking becomes an indispensable tool for problem-solving, decision-making, and innovation, empowering users to tackle the world's most complex challenges.

In conclusion, CoPilot's Deep Thinking application represents a significant step forward in AI capabilities, offering the potential to transform how we approach complex problems, make decisions, and drive innovation. By understanding its core functionalities, potential applications, and challenges, we can harness its power to create a more intelligent and efficient future.

Chapter 8: Compare Deep Thinking vs ChatGPT Deep Research

The landscape of advanced AI is rapidly evolving, with different platforms and applications offering unique capabilities. In this chapter, we'll delve into a comparative analysis of CoPilot's Deep Thinking and ChatGPT's Deep Research, exploring their similarities, differences, strengths, and weaknesses. Understanding these distinctions is crucial for users to leverage the right tool for the right task.

Imagine two powerful AI assistants, each with its own approach to tackling complex challenges and providing in-depth analysis. CoPilot's Deep Thinking and ChatGPT's Deep Research represent distinct approaches to advanced AI, and comparing them will highlight the nuances of their functionalities.

ChatGPT's Deep Research: An Overview

ChatGPT, developed by OpenAI, has gained widespread recognition for its ability to generate human-like text, answer questions, and engage in conversations. Its Deep Research capabilities build upon this foundation, aiming to provide users with more in-depth and comprehensive information on a given topic.

ChatGPT's Deep Research often involves:

- **Information Synthesis:** ChatGPT can gather information from various sources and synthesize it into a coherent and comprehensive response.

- **Text Generation:** ChatGPT excels at generating text, providing detailed explanations, summaries, and analyses.

- **Conversational Interaction:** ChatGPT maintains a conversational tone, allowing users to ask follow-up questions and refine their queries.

CoPilot's Deep Thinking: An Overview

As discussed in the previous chapter, CoPilot's Deep Thinking application focuses on:

- **Complex Problem Solving:** CoPilot Deep Thinking is designed to tackle complex problems that require analysis, reasoning, and hypothesis generation.

- **Advanced Reasoning:** CoPilot Deep Thinking emphasizes deductive, inductive, and abductive reasoning.

- **In-Depth Analysis:** CoPilot Deep Thinking is geared towards analyzing complex datasets and identifying patterns and trends.

Key Differences Between Deep Thinking and ChatGPT Deep Research

While both CoPilot's Deep Thinking and ChatGPT's Deep Research aim to provide advanced AI capabilities, there are key differences in their approach and strengths:

- **Focus:** ChatGPT Deep Research primarily focuses on providing comprehensive information and generating text-based responses. CoPilot Deep Thinking emphasizes problem-solving, analysis, and reasoning.

- **Methodology:** ChatGPT Deep Research relies heavily on its ability to synthesize information and generate text. CoPilot Deep Thinking incorporates more advanced reasoning and analytical capabilities.

- **Output:** ChatGPT Deep Research typically provides text-based outputs, such as summaries, explanations, and analyses. CoPilot Deep Thinking may provide more varied outputs, including analyses, solutions, and hypotheses.

Strengths and Weaknesses

Each approach has its own strengths and weaknesses:

- **ChatGPT Deep Research Strengths:**

- Excellent text generation and summarization.
- Strong conversational capabilities.
- Wide range of knowledge and information.

- **ChatGPT Deep Research Weaknesses:**
  - May sometimes generate inaccurate or misleading information.
  - Can struggle with complex problem-solving that requires more than information retrieval.

- **CoPilot Deep Thinking Strengths:**
  - Stronger analytical and reasoning capabilities.
  - Designed for complex problem-solving.
  - Potential for hypothesis generation and in-depth analysis.

- **CoPilot Deep Thinking Weaknesses:**
  - May not be as strong in text generation and conversational interaction as ChatGPT.
  - The effectiveness may depend heavily on the specific application and the complexity of the problem.

Use Cases and Applications

The choice between CoPilot Deep Thinking and ChatGPT Deep Research may depend on the specific use case:

- Use ChatGPT Deep Research for:
    - Gathering comprehensive information on a topic.
    - Generating summaries and explanations.
    - Engaging in conversational interactions.

- Use CoPilot Deep Thinking for:
    - Tackling complex problems that require analysis and reasoning.
    - Analyzing complex datasets and identifying trends.
    - Generating hypotheses and exploring different scenarios.

Examples

Here are some examples to illustrate the differences:

- Researching a historical event: ChatGPT Deep Research might provide a detailed narrative of the event, including key figures, dates, and causes. CoPilot Deep Thinking might analyze the event in the context of broader historical trends, identify underlying factors, and generate hypotheses about its long-term impact.

- Solving a complex business problem: ChatGPT Deep Research might provide information about different approaches to the problem and summarize relevant case studies. CoPilot Deep Thinking might analyze the problem, identify key factors, generate potential solutions, and evaluate their potential outcomes.

The Future of Advanced AI

Both CoPilot Deep Thinking and ChatGPT Deep Research represent important steps in the evolution of advanced AI. As AI technology continues to advance, we can expect to see even more sophisticated capabilities, greater accuracy, and more seamless integration of different approaches.

The future may involve a convergence of these strengths, with AI systems that can both provide comprehensive information and engage in complex reasoning and problem-solving.

Conclusion

CoPilot Deep Thinking and ChatGPT Deep Research offer distinct approaches to advanced AI, each with its own strengths and weaknesses. Understanding these differences is crucial for users to choose the right tool for the task at hand. By leveraging the unique capabilities of each platform, users can unlock new levels of productivity, insight, and innovation.

Chapter 9: Compare CoPilot Deep Thinking vs Gemini Deep Research

The field of artificial intelligence is a dynamic and competitive space, with various companies and organizations developing their own advanced AI systems. In this chapter, we'll shift our focus to a comparison between CoPilot's Deep Thinking and Gemini's Deep Research. Gemini, developed by Google, represents another significant player in the AI arena. Understanding the distinctions between these two advanced AI approaches will provide further insights into the diverse capabilities of modern AI.

Imagine two powerful AI systems, CoPilot's Deep Thinking and Google's Gemini, each offering unique strengths and approaches to complex problem-solving and information analysis. This chapter will explore their key differences and similarities, highlighting the evolving landscape of AI.

Gemini Deep Research: An Overview

Gemini, developed by Google, is a multimodal AI model, meaning it's designed to understand and operate across different types of information, including text, code, audio, image, and video. Gemini's Deep Research capabilities leverage this multimodal foundation to provide users with comprehensive and nuanced insights.

Gemini's Deep Research often involves:

- **Multimodal Analysis:** Gemini can analyze information across different modalities, such as text, images, and code, providing a more holistic understanding of a topic.

- **Information Retrieval and Synthesis:** Gemini can efficiently retrieve information from a vast range of sources and synthesize it into a coherent and insightful response.

- **Contextual Understanding:** Gemini is designed to have a strong understanding of context, allowing it to provide more relevant and nuanced information.

CoPilot Deep Thinking: An Overview

As we've discussed, CoPilot's Deep Thinking application focuses on:

- **Complex Problem Solving:** CoPilot Deep Thinking is geared towards tackling complex problems that require analysis, reasoning, and hypothesis generation.

- **Advanced Reasoning:** CoPilot Deep Thinking emphasizes deductive, inductive, and abductive reasoning.

- **In-Depth Analysis:** CoPilot Deep Thinking is designed to analyze complex datasets and identify patterns and trends.

Key Differences Between Deep Thinking and Gemini Deep Research

While both CoPilot's Deep Thinking and Gemini's Deep Research are designed to provide advanced AI capabilities, they have key differences in their approach and strengths:

- **Multimodality:** A key differentiator for Gemini is its multimodality. Gemini is designed to understand and operate across different types of information, while CoPilot Deep Thinking may be more focused on text and code analysis.

- **Focus:** Gemini Deep Research emphasizes multimodal analysis, information retrieval, and contextual understanding. CoPilot Deep Thinking focuses on problem-solving, advanced reasoning, and in-depth analysis.

- Application: Gemini may be particularly strong in applications that require multimodal understanding, such as image and video analysis. CoPilot Deep Thinking may be particularly strong in applications that require complex reasoning and problem-solving.

Strengths and Weaknesses

Each approach has its own strengths and weaknesses:

- Gemini Deep Research Strengths:
  - Strong multimodal analysis capabilities.
  - Excellent information retrieval and synthesis.
  - Strong contextual understanding.
- Gemini Deep Research Weaknesses:
  - May not be as focused on complex reasoning and problem-solving as CoPilot Deep Thinking.
  - Effectiveness may depend on the specific application and the availability of multimodal data.
- CoPilot Deep Thinking Strengths:

- Stronger analytical and reasoning capabilities.
- Designed for complex problem-solving.
- Potential for hypothesis generation and in-depth analysis.

- **CoPilot Deep Thinking Weaknesses:**

  - May not be as strong in multimodal analysis as Gemini.
  - Effectiveness may depend heavily on the specific application and the complexity of the problem.

Use Cases and Applications

The choice between CoPilot Deep Thinking and Gemini Deep Research may depend on the specific use case:

- **Use Gemini Deep Research for:**

  - Tasks that require multimodal analysis, such as image and video analysis.
  - Gathering comprehensive information from diverse sources.
  - Understanding complex topics in a contextualized manner.

- **Use CoPilot Deep Thinking for:**

- Tackling complex problems that require analysis and reasoning.

- Analyzing complex datasets and identifying trends.

- Generating hypotheses and exploring different scenarios.

Examples

Here are some examples to illustrate the differences:

- **Analyzing a news event: Gemini Deep Research could analyze the news report, related images and videos, and social media discussions to provide a comprehensive and contextualized understanding of the event. CoPilot Deep Thinking could analyze the event's underlying causes, potential consequences, and implications for policy-making.**

- **Developing a new product: Gemini Deep Research could analyze market trends, consumer feedback, and competitor products across different modalities to identify opportunities for innovation. CoPilot Deep Thinking could analyze the technical challenges, design constraints, and potential risks associated with developing the new product.**

The Future of Multimodal AI

Gemini's emphasis on multimodality represents a significant trend in the evolution of AI. As AI models become increasingly capable of understanding and integrating different types of information, we can expect to see a wider range of applications and more sophisticated AI-driven solutions.

The future may involve a convergence of strengths, with AI systems that can both perform multimodal analysis and engage in complex reasoning and problem-solving.

Conclusion

CoPilot Deep Thinking and Gemini Deep Research offer distinct approaches to advanced AI, with Gemini's strength in multimodality and CoPilot's emphasis on complex reasoning. Understanding these differences is crucial for users to leverage the right AI tool for the right task. By embracing the diverse capabilities of these platforms, we can unlock new possibilities for innovation, discovery, and problem-solving.

Chapter 10: Compare Deep Thinking vs Perplexity Deep Research

The landscape of AI-powered research and information retrieval is constantly evolving, with new platforms and approaches emerging to enhance our ability to access and understand information. In this chapter, we'll compare CoPilot's Deep Thinking to Perplexity's Deep Research, exploring how these two AI systems approach the challenge of providing users with in-depth and reliable information. Understanding their differences will further illuminate the diverse ways in which AI is being applied to research and knowledge discovery.

Imagine two AI systems, CoPilot's Deep Thinking and Perplexity, each designed to empower users with advanced research capabilities. This chapter will delve into their unique features, strengths, and weaknesses, providing a comparative analysis of their approaches to deep research.

Perplexity Deep Research: An Overview

Perplexity is an AI-powered answer engine that aims to provide users with accurate and comprehensive answers to their questions. It distinguishes itself by providing citations and sources for its responses, promoting transparency and allowing users to verify the information.

Perplexity's Deep Research often involves:

- **Answer Engine Functionality:** Perplexity focuses on providing direct answers to user questions, rather than simply providing a list of search results.

- **Citation and Sourcing:** A key feature of Perplexity is its emphasis on providing citations and sources for its responses, enhancing credibility and transparency.

- **Conversational Search:** Perplexity allows for a more conversational search experience, enabling users to ask follow-up questions and refine their queries.

CoPilot Deep Thinking: An Overview

As we've discussed, CoPilot's Deep Thinking application focuses on:

- **Complex Problem Solving:** CoPilot Deep Thinking is geared towards tackling complex problems that require analysis, reasoning, and hypothesis generation.

- **Advanced Reasoning:** CoPilot Deep Thinking emphasizes deductive, inductive, and abductive reasoning.

- **In-Depth Analysis:** CoPilot Deep Thinking is designed to analyze complex datasets and identify patterns and trends.

Key Differences Between Deep Thinking and Perplexity Deep Research

While both CoPilot's Deep Thinking and Perplexity Deep Research aim to provide advanced AI capabilities, they have key differences in their approach and strengths:

- **Focus:** Perplexity Deep Research primarily focuses on providing direct answers to questions with citations and sources. CoPilot Deep Thinking emphasizes problem-solving, advanced reasoning, and in-depth analysis.

- **Methodology:** Perplexity Deep Research relies heavily on its ability to synthesize information and provide answers with citations. CoPilot Deep Thinking incorporates more advanced reasoning and analytical capabilities.

- **Output:** Perplexity Deep Research typically provides direct answers with citations and sources. CoPilot Deep Thinking may provide more varied outputs, including analyses, solutions, and hypotheses.

Strengths and Weaknesses

Each approach has its own strengths and weaknesses:

- **Perplexity Deep Research Strengths:**
    - Provides direct answers to questions.
    - Emphasizes citation and sourcing, enhancing credibility.

- Offers a conversational search experience.

- **Perplexity Deep Research Weaknesses:**
  - May be less focused on complex problem-solving and in-depth analysis compared to CoPilot Deep Thinking.
  - Effectiveness may depend on the availability of reliable sources for the query.

- **CoPilot Deep Thinking Strengths:**
  - Stronger analytical and reasoning capabilities.
  - Designed for complex problem-solving.
  - Potential for hypothesis generation and in-depth analysis.

- **CoPilot Deep Thinking Weaknesses:**
  - May not be as focused on providing direct answers with citations as Perplexity.
  - The effectiveness may depend heavily on the specific application and the complexity of the problem.

Use Cases and Applications

The choice between CoPilot Deep Thinking and Perplexity Deep Research may depend on the specific use case:

- Use Perplexity Deep Research for:

    o Finding direct answers to specific questions.

    o Conducting research that requires reliable sources and citations.

    o Engaging in a conversational search experience.

- Use CoPilot Deep Thinking for:

    o Tackling complex problems that require analysis and reasoning.

    o Analyzing complex datasets and identifying trends.

    o Generating hypotheses and exploring different scenarios.

Examples

Here are some examples to illustrate the differences:

- Researching the effects of climate change: Perplexity Deep Research might provide direct answers to questions about the causes, effects, and potential solutions to climate change, with citations to scientific studies and reports. CoPilot Deep Thinking might analyze climate data, model potential future scenarios, and generate hypotheses about the long-term impact of climate change on different regions.

- Analyzing a business trend: Perplexity Deep Research might provide information about the key players, market size, and growth potential of a particular business trend, with citations to market research reports and industry publications. CoPilot Deep Thinking might analyze the underlying factors driving the trend, identify potential opportunities and risks, and generate strategies for businesses to capitalize on the trend.

The Importance of Transparency and Reliability in AI Research

Perplexity's emphasis on citation and sourcing highlights the growing importance of transparency and reliability in AI-powered research. As AI systems play an increasingly important role in information retrieval and knowledge discovery, it's crucial that they provide users with the ability to verify the information they provide.

The future of AI research will likely involve a combination of different approaches, with systems that can both provide direct answers with citations and engage in complex reasoning and analysis.

Conclusion

CoPilot Deep Thinking and Perplexity Deep Research offer distinct approaches to advanced AI research, with Perplexity's strength in providing direct answers with citations and CoPilot's emphasis on complex reasoning and analysis. Understanding these differences is crucial for users to choose the right AI tool for their research needs. By leveraging the unique capabilities of these platforms, we can enhance our ability to access, understand, and utilize information in a more effective and reliable way.

Chapter 11: Upload Documents with Deep Thinking

In the modern world, information is often stored and shared in various document formats. From reports and research papers to legal contracts and business proposals, documents are a cornerstone of how we communicate and work. CoPilot's Deep Thinking capabilities can be significantly enhanced by the ability to upload and analyze these documents. This chapter explores the integration of document uploading with Deep Thinking, examining its benefits, use cases, and the transformative potential it brings to information processing and analysis.

Imagine CoPilot's Deep Thinking not just working with general knowledge but also being able to analyze your specific documents, extracting insights, answering questions, and performing complex analyses tailored to your unique information. That's the power of integrating document uploads with Deep Thinking.

The Importance of Document Processing in AI

Document processing is a critical aspect of AI development. It involves enabling AI systems to:

- **Understand Document Structure:** AI needs to be able to recognize different elements within a document, such as headings, paragraphs, tables, and images.

- **Extract Information:** AI needs to be able to extract relevant information from documents, such as key data, facts, and conclusions.

- **Analyze Content:** AI needs to be able to analyze the content of documents, identify patterns, and draw meaningful insights.

By enabling CoPilot's Deep Thinking to process uploaded documents, we unlock a wide range of new possibilities for information analysis and utilization.

How Document Uploading Enhances Deep Thinking

Uploading documents to CoPilot's Deep Thinking enhances its capabilities in several key ways:

- **Contextual Analysis:** Uploaded documents provide CoPilot with specific context, allowing it to perform analyses that are tailored to the user's unique information.

- **Targeted Information Retrieval:** Users can ask CoPilot specific questions about the content of their uploaded documents, enabling efficient and targeted information retrieval.

- **Customized Analysis:** Deep Thinking can perform customized analyses on uploaded documents, such as identifying key themes, summarizing key findings, and comparing different sections.

- **Data Extraction:** CoPilot can extract data from uploaded documents, such as tables and lists, and use that data for further analysis or processing.

- **Workflow Integration:** Document uploading can seamlessly integrate CoPilot Deep Thinking into existing workflows, allowing users to analyze their documents without having to switch between different applications.

Use Cases for Uploading Documents with Deep Thinking

The ability to upload documents with CoPilot Deep Thinking opens up a wide range of use cases across different fields:

- **Research and Analysis: Researchers can upload research papers, articles, and reports to CoPilot to analyze findings, identify trends, and generate new hypotheses.**

- **Legal Review: Lawyers can upload legal documents, such as contracts and court filings, to CoPilot to review terms, identify potential risks, and conduct legal research.**

- **Business Intelligence: Businesses can upload business reports, market analyses, and financial statements to CoPilot to gain insights into performance, identify opportunities, and make informed decisions.**

- **Education: Students can upload lecture notes, textbooks, and research papers to CoPilot to summarize key concepts, answer questions, and prepare for exams.**

- **Personal Productivity: Individuals can upload personal documents, such as meeting notes, to-do lists, and project plans, to CoPilot to organize information, track progress, and manage tasks.**

Examples of Document Uploads with Deep Thinking in Action

Here are some examples of how uploading documents with CoPilot Deep Thinking might be used:

- A researcher uploads a collection of scientific papers to CoPilot and asks it to identify the key trends in the field and generate a summary of the latest research findings.

- A lawyer uploads a complex legal contract to CoPilot and asks it to identify the key clauses, highlight any potential risks, and generate a summary of the contract's terms.

- A business analyst uploads a market research report to CoPilot and asks it to extract the key market trends, identify the major competitors, and generate a SWOT analysis.

- A student uploads their lecture notes to CoPilot and asks it to summarize the key concepts, generate practice questions, and create a study guide.

Challenges and Considerations

While uploading documents with Deep Thinking offers significant benefits, there are also challenges and considerations:

- Document Format Compatibility: CoPilot needs to be able to process a wide range of document formats, including PDFs, Word documents, and text files.

- Data Security and Privacy: It's crucial to ensure the security and privacy of uploaded documents, protecting sensitive information from unauthorized access.

- Accuracy and Reliability: The accuracy and reliability of Deep Thinking's analysis will depend on the quality and clarity of the uploaded documents.

- Handling Complex Documents: CoPilot needs to be able to handle complex documents with various formatting and structures, such as tables, images, and embedded objects.

The Future of Document Processing with AI

The future of document processing with AI is bright, with ongoing advancements in AI technology and natural language processing. We can expect to see even more sophisticated capabilities, such as:

- Advanced Document Understanding: AI will become even better at understanding the nuances of document content, including sentiment, intent, and context.

- **Automated Document Workflows:** AI will be able to automate complex document workflows, such as document classification, routing, and approval.

- **Integration with Other AI Systems:** Document processing capabilities will be seamlessly integrated with other AI systems, such as chatbots, virtual assistants, and data analytics platforms.

Conclusion

Uploading documents with CoPilot Deep Thinking unlocks a powerful new dimension in AI-driven information analysis. By enabling CoPilot to process and understand specific documents, we can tailor its capabilities to our unique needs, enhancing productivity, improving decision-making, and transforming the way we work with information. As AI technology continues to advance, the potential for document processing with Deep Thinking is limitless, paving the way for a future where AI empowers us to extract maximum value from our information.

Chapter 12: Creating Images with CoPilot

The intersection of artificial intelligence and creative expression is rapidly evolving, with AI systems now capable of generating not just text, but also images. CoPilot, in its expanding capabilities, is venturing into this realm, allowing users to create visual content through simple prompts and instructions. This chapter explores the image generation capabilities of CoPilot, examining how it works, its potential applications, and the transformative impact it has on the creative process.

Imagine CoPilot transforming from an assistant that primarily works with text to a creative partner that can bring your visual ideas to life. That's the exciting potential of creating images with CoPilot.

The Rise of AI Image Generation

AI image generation is a field that has seen remarkable progress in recent years. AI models, often based on deep learning techniques like generative adversarial networks (GANs) and diffusion models, are now capable of creating highly realistic and imaginative images. These models learn from vast datasets of images, enabling them to understand visual concepts, styles, and compositions, and then generate new images based on user input.

CoPilot's integration of image generation capabilities represents a significant step in making this technology more accessible and user-friendly. It's about empowering users to express their creativity and visualize their ideas without needing specialized artistic skills or complex software.

How CoPilot Draws Images

CoPilot utilizes advanced AI models to generate images based on user prompts. The process typically involves the following steps:

1. Prompt Input: The user provides CoPilot with a text-based prompt describing the image they want to create. This prompt can be as simple as a few keywords or as detailed as a paragraph describing the desired scene, style, and composition.

2. Prompt Interpretation: CoPilot's AI model interprets the user's prompt, understanding the visual concepts, styles, and details described.

3. Image Generation: The AI model generates an image based on its understanding of the prompt. This involves creating the image from scratch,

synthesizing visual elements, and applying artistic styles.

4. Image Output: CoPilot presents the generated image to the user. Depending on the system, users may be able to refine the image, generate variations, or download the image for use in their projects.

Potential Applications of Creating Images with CoPilot

The ability to draw images with CoPilot has a wide range of potential applications across various fields:

- Creative Content Creation: CoPilot can be used to generate images for various creative projects, such as illustrations for books, artwork for websites, and visual designs for marketing materials.

- Design and Prototyping: CoPilot can help designers visualize and prototype their ideas, generating images of products, interiors, and architectural designs based on their concepts.

- Storyboarding and Visualization: CoPilot can be used to create storyboards for films, animations, and video games, allowing creators to visualize scenes and characters.

- Education and Learning: CoPilot can be used to generate images for educational materials, making complex concepts more visually engaging and easier to understand.

- Accessibility: CoPilot can help people with visual impairments or artistic limitations express their creativity and visualize their ideas.

Examples of Drawing Images with CoPilot in Action

Here are some examples of how drawing images with CoPilot might be used:

- A writer uses CoPilot to generate illustrations for their children's book, describing the characters and scenes in their stories and having CoPilot bring them to life visually.

- A graphic designer uses CoPilot to create a range of design options for a website, experimenting with different styles and compositions based on their client's brief.

- An architect uses CoPilot to generate visualizations of a building design, allowing clients to see what the finished project will look like before construction begins.

- A teacher uses CoPilot to create custom images for a presentation, making their lessons more engaging and visually appealing for their students.

Challenges and Considerations

While drawing images with CoPilot offers exciting possibilities, there are also challenges and considerations:

- **Prompt Engineering:** The quality of the generated image depends heavily on the quality of the user's prompt. Users may need to learn how to effectively describe their desired image to get the best results.

- **Artistic Control:** While CoPilot can generate images, users may have limited control over the specific details and artistic style of the generated image.

- **Ethical Implications:** AI image generation raises ethical considerations related to copyright, ownership, and the potential for misuse.

- **Technological Limitations:** AI image generation technology is still evolving, and there may be limitations in the types of images that CoPilot can generate or the level of detail and realism that can be achieved.

The Future of AI Image Generation

The future of AI image generation is full of potential. As AI models continue to improve, we can expect to see:

- **More Realistic and Detailed Images:** AI will be able to generate even more realistic and detailed images, approaching the quality of professional artwork.

- **Increased User Control:** Users will have more control over the creative process, being able to refine and customize generated images to a greater extent.

- **Integration with Other Creative Tools:** AI image generation will be seamlessly integrated with other creative tools, such as image editing software and design platforms.

- **New Forms of Artistic Expression:** AI image generation will open up new possibilities for artistic expression, allowing creators to explore new styles and techniques.

Conclusion

Creating images with CoPilot represents a significant step forward in the democratization of creativity. By empowering users to generate visual content through simple prompts, CoPilot is making AI image generation more accessible and user-friendly. As this technology continues to evolve, it has the potential to transform the way we create, design, and express ourselves, opening up new frontiers in artistic exploration and visual communication.

Chapter 13: CoPilot Labs

In the ever-evolving world of artificial intelligence, innovation is key. Companies often establish "labs" or similar initiatives to explore cutting-edge technologies, experiment with new ideas, and push the boundaries of what's possible. CoPilot, in its pursuit of advancing AI capabilities, likely has a similar space for experimentation and development. This chapter delves into the concept of "CoPilot Labs" (or its equivalent), exploring its purpose, potential activities, and the role it plays in shaping the future of CoPilot.

Imagine a hub of innovation where CoPilot's developers and researchers are constantly exploring new frontiers in AI, pushing the limits of what CoPilot can do. That's the essence of CoPilot Labs.

The Purpose of CoPilot Labs

CoPilot Labs, or its equivalent within Microsoft, serves several key purposes:

- Research and Development: CoPilot Labs is a space for conducting research into new AI technologies, exploring emerging trends, and developing innovative solutions.

- Experimentation and Prototyping: It's a place for experimenting with new features, functionalities, and applications of CoPilot, creating prototypes, and testing their feasibility.

- Exploration of Emerging Technologies: CoPilot Labs focuses on exploring emerging technologies, such as advanced machine learning techniques, natural language processing advancements, and new forms of human-computer interaction.

- Pushing the Boundaries of AI: The labs aim to push the boundaries of what AI can do, exploring new capabilities and applications that can transform how we interact with technology.

- **Future-Proofing CoPilot:** CoPilot Labs plays a crucial role in future-proofing CoPilot, ensuring it stays at the forefront of AI innovation and remains competitive in the market.

Potential Activities in CoPilot Labs

The activities within CoPilot Labs can be diverse and dynamic, including:

- **Developing New AI Models:** Researchers may be working on developing new AI models with enhanced capabilities, such as improved understanding of natural language, more advanced reasoning, and better ability to generate creative content.

- **Exploring Multimodal AI:** CoPilot Labs may be exploring multimodal AI, integrating different types of information, such as text, images, audio, and video, to create more comprehensive and intuitive AI experiences.

- **Experimenting with Human-Computer Interaction:** Researchers may be experimenting with new ways for humans to interact with CoPilot, such as through voice, gestures, and brain-computer interfaces.

- Investigating Ethical Considerations: CoPilot Labs may also be involved in investigating the ethical implications of AI, ensuring that CoPilot is developed and used responsibly.

- Prototyping New Applications: Developers may be prototyping new applications of CoPilot, exploring how it can be used in different industries and domains.

Examples of Potential CoPilot Labs Projects

Here are some examples of potential projects that might be undertaken in CoPilot Labs:

- Developing an AI model that can understand and respond to human emotions, creating a more empathetic and personalized AI experience.

- Exploring the integration of CoPilot with augmented reality (AR) and virtual reality (VR) technologies, creating immersive and interactive AI experiences.

- Experimenting with new ways to use CoPilot to enhance creativity, such as by generating music, art, and other forms of creative content.

- Investigating the use of CoPilot to address social challenges, such as improving access to education, healthcare, and other essential services.

The Role of CoPilot Labs in Shaping the Future of CoPilot

CoPilot Labs plays a crucial role in shaping the future of CoPilot by:

- **Driving Innovation:** CoPilot Labs is the engine of innovation, pushing the boundaries of what CoPilot can do and exploring new possibilities for AI.

- **Developing New Features and Capabilities:** The research and development conducted in CoPilot Labs will lead to the development of new features and capabilities that will enhance the user experience.

- **Expanding the Applications of CoPilot:** CoPilot Labs will explore new applications of CoPilot, expanding its reach and impact across different industries and domains.

- **Ensuring CoPilot's Competitiveness:** By staying at the forefront of AI innovation, CoPilot Labs ensures that CoPilot remains competitive in the rapidly evolving AI landscape.

- **Addressing Ethical Considerations:** CoPilot Labs helps to ensure that CoPilot is developed and used responsibly, addressing ethical considerations and promoting responsible AI practices.

Challenges and Considerations

While CoPilot Labs is essential for innovation, there are also challenges and considerations:

- **Balancing Exploration and Practicality: CoPilot Labs needs to balance the exploration of cutting-edge technologies with the development of practical and useful applications.**

- **Managing Risk: Experimentation and innovation involve risk, and CoPilot Labs needs to manage risk effectively to avoid costly failures.**

- **Translating Research into Products: The research and development conducted in CoPilot Labs needs to be translated into actual products and features that benefit users.**

- **Attracting and Retaining Talent: CoPilot Labs needs to attract and retain top AI talent to drive innovation and achieve its goals.**

The Future of CoPilot Labs

The future of CoPilot Labs is exciting, with the potential to transform the way we interact with technology. As AI technology continues to advance, we can expect to see:

- **More Sophisticated AI Models: CoPilot Labs will develop even more sophisticated AI models with enhanced capabilities.**

- Seamless Integration of AI into Our Lives: The innovations from CoPilot Labs will lead to a more seamless integration of AI into our daily lives, making technology more intuitive and helpful.

- AI-Driven Solutions to Global Challenges: CoPilot Labs may contribute to developing AI-driven solutions to some of the world's most pressing challenges.

Conclusion

CoPilot Labs, or its equivalent, is the driving force behind CoPilot's innovation and development. It's a space for exploration, experimentation, and pushing the boundaries of what AI can do. By investing in research and development, CoPilot Labs is shaping the future of CoPilot and ensuring that it remains a leading force in the AI revolution, transforming how we interact with technology and empowering us to achieve more.

Chapter 14: CoPilot with Bing

In the vast expanse of the internet, search engines serve as our primary gateway to information. Bing, Microsoft's search engine, has been undergoing a significant transformation with the integration of CoPilot. This chapter explores the synergy between CoPilot and Bing, examining how this integration enhances search capabilities, transforms the user experience, and reshapes the landscape of online information retrieval.

Imagine Bing not just as a search engine that delivers links, but as an intelligent assistant that provides comprehensive answers, contextual insights, and interactive experiences. That's the vision behind CoPilot's integration with Bing.

The Evolution of Search Engines

Traditional search engines primarily focused on keyword matching and link ranking. Users would enter a query, and the search engine would return a list of relevant web pages. However, with the advancements in AI, search engines are evolving to provide more intelligent and conversational experiences.

CoPilot's integration with Bing represents a significant step in this evolution, moving beyond simple keyword matching to a more nuanced understanding of user intent and the ability to provide comprehensive and contextually relevant answers.

How CoPilot Enhances Bing

CoPilot enhances Bing in several key ways:

- Conversational Search: CoPilot enables a more conversational search experience, allowing users to ask questions in natural language and engage in follow-up dialogues.

- Comprehensive Answers: CoPilot goes beyond simply providing links, synthesizing information from various sources to provide comprehensive and direct answers to user queries.

- Contextual Understanding: CoPilot's AI model understands the context of user queries, allowing it to provide more relevant and personalized results.

- Summarization and Analysis: CoPilot can summarize and analyze information from web pages and other sources, providing users with concise and insightful summaries.

- Creative Content Generation: CoPilot can generate creative content, such as text summaries, articles, and even code snippets, based on user prompts and search queries.

Use Cases for CoPilot with Bing

The integration of CoPilot with Bing opens up a wide range of use cases:

- **Research and Information Gathering:** Users can use CoPilot to conduct in-depth research on various topics, gathering information from diverse sources and receiving comprehensive summaries.

- **Problem Solving and Decision Making:** CoPilot can assist users in solving problems and making decisions by providing relevant information, analyzing data, and generating potential solutions.

- **Learning and Education:** CoPilot can be used as a learning tool, providing explanations, summaries, and examples to help users understand complex concepts.

- **Travel and Planning:** CoPilot can assist users in planning trips, providing information about destinations, flights, hotels, and local attractions.

- **Entertainment and Recreation:** CoPilot can help users find movies, music, and other forms of entertainment, as well as provide information about local events and activities.

Examples of CoPilot with Bing in Action

Here are some examples of how CoPilot with Bing might be used:

- A student uses CoPilot to research a historical event, asking questions about the causes, effects, and key figures involved.

- A traveler uses CoPilot to plan a trip to a foreign country, asking questions about the best time to visit, local customs, and transportation options.

- A professional uses CoPilot to research a market trend, analyzing data from various sources and generating a summary of the key findings.

- A user asks CoPilot to find a recipe for a specific dish and then asks for ways to modify the recipe for dietary restrictions.

Challenges and Considerations

While CoPilot with Bing offers significant benefits, there are also challenges and considerations:

- Accuracy and Reliability: Ensuring the accuracy and reliability of the information provided by CoPilot is crucial, as users rely on search engines for accurate information.

- Bias and Fairness: AI models can be susceptible to bias, and it's important to address potential biases in CoPilot to ensure fairness and equity in search results.

- **Privacy and Data Security: Protecting user privacy and ensuring data security is essential, as search engines collect and process vast amounts of user data.**

- **Maintaining Relevance: Keeping up with the ever-changing landscape of the internet and ensuring that search results remain relevant and up-to-date is a continuous challenge.**

The Future of Search with AI

The integration of CoPilot with Bing represents a significant step in the evolution of search engines. As AI technology continues to advance, we can expect to see:

- **More Personalized Search Experiences: AI will enable search engines to provide more personalized search experiences, tailoring results to individual user preferences and needs.**

- **Seamless Integration with Other AI Systems: Search engines will be seamlessly integrated with other AI systems, such as virtual assistants and chatbots, creating more comprehensive and intuitive AI experiences.**

- **Enhanced Multimodal Search: AI will enable search engines to understand and process information from various modalities, such as** images, audio, and video, leading to more comprehensive and engaging search results.

- **Proactive Information Retrieval:** AI will enable search engines to proactively provide information that is relevant to users, anticipating their needs and providing timely assistance.

Conclusion

CoPilot's integration with Bing is transforming the search engine experience, moving beyond simple keyword matching to a more conversational, comprehensive, and contextually relevant approach to information retrieval. By leveraging the power of AI, CoPilot with Bing is reshaping the landscape of online information access, empowering users to explore the vast expanse of the internet with greater ease and efficiency. As AI technology continues to evolve, the synergy between CoPilot and Bing will continue to shape the future of search, providing users with more intelligent and intuitive ways to access and understand information.

Chapter 15: Use CoPilot as Voice Search

In a world where speed and convenience are paramount, the ability to interact with technology using our voice is becoming increasingly important. CoPilot's capabilities extend beyond text-based interaction, allowing users to leverage it for "audible search." This chapter explores how CoPilot can be used as an audible search tool, examining its advantages, use cases, and how it transforms the way we access information through voice commands.

Imagine being able to access the vast resources of the internet simply by speaking your questions and commands, without needing to type or interact with a screen. That's the power of using CoPilot as an audible search tool.

The Rise of Voice-Based Interaction

Voice assistants and voice-based search have become increasingly popular, driven by advancements in speech recognition and natural language processing. This technology allows users to interact with devices and access information using their voice, offering a more hands-free and convenient way to use technology.

CoPilot's integration of audible search capabilities aligns with this trend, providing users with a more natural and efficient way to find information, control devices, and perform tasks using voice commands.

How CoPilot Works as Audible Search

CoPilot functions as an audible search tool through the following process:

1. Voice Input: The user provides a search query or command using their voice. CoPilot's speech recognition technology converts the spoken words into text.

2. Query Processing: CoPilot's AI model processes the user's query, understanding the intent and identifying the relevant information or action to be performed.

3. Information Retrieval or Action Execution: CoPilot retrieves relevant information from the web or other sources, or executes the requested action, such as controlling a device or playing media.

4. Audible Output: CoPilot provides the results or response to the user in an audible format, using text-to-speech technology to convert the information into spoken words.

Advantages of Using CoPilot as Audible Search

Using CoPilot as an audible search tool offers several advantages:

- **Hands-Free Convenience:** Audible search allows users to access information and control devices without needing to use their hands, making it convenient for multitasking, driving, or other situations where hands are occupied.

- **Speed and Efficiency:** Voice commands can be faster than typing, allowing users to quickly access information or perform tasks.

- **Accessibility:** Audible search can make technology more accessible to people with disabilities, providing an alternative way to interact with devices and access information.

- **Natural and Intuitive Interaction:** Voice interaction is a natural and intuitive way for humans to communicate, making it easier and more comfortable to interact with technology.

Use Cases for CoPilot as Audible Search

CoPilot can be used as an audible search tool in various situations:

- **Information Retrieval:** Users can ask CoPilot questions and retrieve information from the web using voice commands, such as "What's the weather today?" or "Find me the nearest Italian restaurant."

- Navigation and Directions: CoPilot can provide directions and navigation assistance using voice commands, such as "Navigate to my home" or "Find the nearest gas station."

- Controlling Devices: CoPilot can control smart home devices and other connected devices using voice commands, such as "Turn on the lights" or "Play music."

- Setting Reminders and Alarms: CoPilot can set reminders and alarms using voice commands, such as "Remind me to call John at 5 PM" or "Set an alarm for 7 AM."

- Communication: CoPilot can send messages and make calls using voice commands, such as "Send a message to Sarah saying I'm running late" or "Call John."

Examples of CoPilot Audible Search in Action

Here are some examples of how CoPilot might be used as an audible search tool:

- A driver uses CoPilot to get directions, make calls, and play music while keeping their hands on the wheel and their eyes on the road.

- A person with a visual impairment uses CoPilot to navigate the web, access information, and control their devices using voice commands.

- A busy professional uses CoPilot to set reminders, schedule meetings, and send emails while multitasking.

- A user in the kitchen uses CoPilot to find a recipe, set a timer, and convert measurements using voice commands.

Challenges and Considerations

While CoPilot's audible search capabilities offer many benefits, there are also challenges and considerations:

- Accuracy of Speech Recognition: The accuracy of speech recognition is crucial for effective audible search. CoPilot needs to accurately understand user commands, even in noisy environments or with different accents.

- Natural Language Understanding: CoPilot needs to understand the nuances of natural language, including variations in phrasing, grammar, and vocabulary.

- Contextual Awareness: CoPilot needs to be contextually aware, understanding the user's intent and providing relevant responses based on the situation.

- **Privacy Concerns:** Voice interaction raises privacy concerns, as voice recordings may be stored and processed. It's important to ensure user privacy and data security.

The Future of Audible Search

The future of audible search is promising, with continued advancements in AI and voice technology. We can expect to see:

- **More Natural and Conversational Interaction:** AI will become even better at understanding and responding to natural language, leading to more conversational and intuitive voice interactions.

- **Seamless Integration with AI Assistants:** Audible search will be seamlessly integrated with AI assistants, providing a more comprehensive and personalized AI experience.

- **Enhanced Multimodal Interaction:** Audible search will be combined with other modalities, such as visual and gestural input, creating more rich and interactive user experiences.

- **Proactive Voice Assistance:** AI assistants will become more proactive, anticipating user needs and providing timely assistance based on context and preferences.

Conclusion

Using CoPilot as an audible search tool offers a more convenient, efficient, and accessible way to interact with technology and access information. By leveraging the power of voice, CoPilot is transforming the way we search, control devices, and perform tasks, making technology more intuitive and user-friendly. As AI and voice technology continue to advance, the potential for CoPilot as an audible search tool is limitless, paving the way for a future where our voices become the primary interface to our digital world.

Chapter 16: Request Citations From Written Queries

In the realm of research, information gathering, and academic writing, the ability to verify sources and ensure the credibility of information is paramount. CoPilot, in its role as an AI assistant, can enhance its utility by providing citations for the information it presents in response to user queries. This chapter explores the capability of requesting citations from CoPilot through written queries, examining its importance, how it works, and its impact on the reliability and transparency of AI-generated information.

Imagine CoPilot not only providing you with answers but also giving you the ability to trace those answers back to their original sources, allowing you to verify their accuracy and explore the topic further. That's the power of requesting citations from CoPilot.

The Importance of Citations in Information Retrieval

Citations play a crucial role in information retrieval and research:

- **Verifying Information: Citations allow users to verify the accuracy and credibility of information by referencing the original sources.**

- **Establishing Authority: Citations help to establish the authority and expertise of the sources used, providing context and credibility to the information presented.**

- **Avoiding Plagiarism: In academic and professional settings, citations are essential to avoid plagiarism and give credit to the original authors.**

- **Facilitating Further Research: Citations provide users with a pathway to explore the topic further, allowing them to delve deeper into the original sources and expand their knowledge.**

By enabling users to request citations from CoPilot, we enhance the reliability and transparency of AI-generated information, making it more suitable for research, academic writing, and other applications where source verification is critical.

How CoPilot Provides Citations

CoPilot, when equipped with the ability to provide citations, typically works through the following process:

1. Query Input: The user provides a written query to CoPilot, requesting information on a specific topic.

2. Information Retrieval: CoPilot's AI model retrieves relevant information from various sources, such as web pages, databases, and other knowledge repositories.

3. Source Identification: CoPilot identifies the sources from which the retrieved information originated, noting the specific URLs, publications, or other references.

4. Citation Generation: CoPilot generates citations for the identified sources, formatting them according to a specific citation style, such as APA, MLA, or Chicago.

5. Response Output: CoPilot presents the response to the user, including the requested information along with the generated citations.

Benefits of Requesting Citations from CoPilot

Requesting citations from CoPilot offers several benefits:

- **Enhanced Reliability:** Providing citations enhances the reliability of the information provided by CoPilot, allowing users to verify its accuracy and credibility.

- **Increased Transparency:** Citations increase the transparency of the AI's information retrieval process, allowing users to see where the information originated.

- **Improved Research Capabilities:** The ability to request citations makes CoPilot a more valuable tool for research, enabling users to gather information and verify its sources efficiently.

- **Support for Academic Writing:** Citations are essential in academic writing, and CoPilot's ability to provide them supports students, researchers, and scholars in their writing process.

- **Reduced Risk of Misinformation:** By providing citations, CoPilot can help to reduce the risk of users relying on inaccurate or misleading information.

Use Cases for Requesting Citations from CoPilot

Requesting citations from CoPilot is useful in various situations:

- **Academic Research:** Students and researchers can use CoPilot to gather information for their research projects, ensuring that they have access to reliable sources and can properly cite their work.

- **Fact-Checking:** Users can request citations to verify the accuracy of information they encounter online or in other sources, helping them to identify misinformation.

- **Professional Writing:** Writers and journalists can use CoPilot to gather information for their articles and reports, ensuring that they can properly cite their sources and maintain journalistic integrity.

- **Legal Research:** Lawyers and legal professionals can use CoPilot to research legal precedents and case law, ensuring that they have access to reliable sources and can properly cite their legal documents.

- **Information Gathering for Decision-Making:** Users can request citations to gather information for important decisions, ensuring that they have access to credible sources and can make informed choices.

Examples of Requesting Citations from CoPilot in Action

Here are some examples of how requesting citations from CoPilot might be used:

- A student asks CoPilot, "Explain the causes of World War I," and then requests citations to verify the information and find sources for their research paper.

- A journalist asks CoPilot, "What are the latest developments in artificial intelligence?" and then requests citations to support their article and ensure accuracy.

- A researcher asks CoPilot, "Summarize the findings of this scientific study," and then requests citations to delve deeper into the original research.

- A user asks CoPilot, "What are the health benefits of exercise?" and then requests citations to find credible sources for the information.

Challenges and Considerations

While the ability to request citations from CoPilot offers significant benefits, there are also challenges and considerations:

- Accuracy of Citations: Ensuring the accuracy and completeness of citations is crucial. CoPilot needs to accurately identify the original sources and format the citations correctly.

- **Attribution of Information:** Determining the precise origin of information can be complex, especially when information is synthesized from multiple sources. CoPilot needs to attribute information accurately and avoid plagiarism.

- **Citation Style Formatting:** CoPilot needs to be able to format citations according to various citation styles, such as APA, MLA, and Chicago, to meet the specific requirements of different contexts.

- **Handling Complex Sources:** CoPilot needs to be able to handle complex sources, such as books, articles, websites, and databases, and generate citations that are appropriate for each type of source.

The Future of Citations in AI-Generated Information

The ability to request citations from AI systems like CoPilot is likely to become increasingly important as AI plays a larger role in information retrieval and knowledge generation. We can expect to see:

- **More Sophisticated Citation Systems:** AI systems will develop more sophisticated citation systems, capable of handling a wider range of sources and formatting citations with greater accuracy.

- Integration of Citation Metadata: AI systems will integrate citation metadata, such as author information, publication dates, and source credibility ratings, to provide users with more comprehensive information about the sources.

- Automated Citation Generation: AI systems will automate the process of citation generation, making it easier for users to verify information and create accurate citations.

- Emphasis on Transparency and Accountability: The ability to request citations will become a standard feature in AI-powered information retrieval, emphasizing transparency and accountability in AI-generated information.

Conclusion

Requesting citations from written CoPilot queries enhances the reliability, transparency, and utility of AI-generated information. By providing users with the ability to verify sources and trace information back to its origin, CoPilot becomes a more valuable tool for research, academic writing, and any context where source verification is critical.

Chapter 17: Using CoPilot as a Journal

In an age of digital transformation, the traditional practice of journaling is evolving. CoPilot, with its advanced AI capabilities, offers a unique opportunity to enhance and transform the journaling experience. This chapter explores the potential of using CoPilot as a journal, examining its advantages, various applications, and how it can revolutionize the way we document our thoughts, experiences, and reflections.

Imagine CoPilot not just as an assistant for tasks and information, but as a supportive companion for your personal reflections, helping you capture memories, analyze thoughts, and gain insights from your own journal entries. That's the potential of using CoPilot as a journal.

The Evolution of Journaling

Journaling has been a long-standing practice for self-reflection, personal growth, and documentation of life experiences. Traditionally, journaling involved writing in a physical notebook. However, with the rise of digital technology, journaling has expanded to include various formats, such as:

- **Digital Documents:** Using word processors or text editors to create and store journal entries.

- **Journaling Apps:** Dedicated apps designed specifically for journaling, offering features like tagging, search, and multimedia integration.

- **Blogs and Online Platforms:** Sharing journal entries publicly or privately on online platforms.

CoPilot offers a new dimension to this evolution, bringing the power of AI to enhance the journaling process in ways that were previously unimaginable.

Advantages of Using CoPilot as a Journal

Using CoPilot as a journal offers several advantages:

- **Enhanced Organization:** CoPilot can help organize journal entries with tagging, categorization, and automatic dating, making it easier to search and retrieve specific entries.

- **Improved Reflection:** CoPilot can analyze journal entries to identify patterns, themes, and emotions, providing users with deeper insights into their thoughts and feelings.

- **Creative Writing Assistance:** CoPilot can assist with creative writing, helping users to express their thoughts and feelings in more descriptive and evocative language.

- Multimedia Integration: CoPilot can facilitate the integration of multimedia elements into journal entries, such as images, audio recordings, and videos.

- Privacy and Security: CoPilot can provide enhanced privacy and security for journal entries, ensuring that personal information is protected.

How CoPilot Can Enhance the Journaling Experience

CoPilot can enhance the journaling experience in several ways:

- Prompt Generation: CoPilot can provide prompts and writing suggestions to help users overcome writer's block and explore new topics for reflection.

- Entry Analysis: CoPilot can analyze journal entries to identify keywords, sentiment, and recurring themes, providing users with a summary of their emotional state and key topics.

- Progress Tracking: CoPilot can track progress over time, visualizing changes in mood, identifying personal growth, and highlighting areas for improvement.

- Goal Setting and Tracking: CoPilot can help users set personal goals and track their progress, providing reminders, encouragement, and insights to stay motivated.

- **Accessibility Features:** CoPilot can provide accessibility features for users with disabilities, such as voice input, text-to-speech, and customizable font sizes.

Use Cases for Using CoPilot as a Journal

CoPilot can be used as a journal in various situations:

- **Personal Reflection:** Users can use CoPilot to document their daily experiences, thoughts, and feelings, providing a space for self-reflection and personal growth.

- **Creative Writing:** Writers can use CoPilot as a tool for creative writing, exploring different styles, experimenting with language, and developing their writing skills.

- **Therapeutic Journaling:** Individuals engaged in therapy can use CoPilot to document their sessions, track their progress, and gain insights into their emotional and mental well-being.

- **Travel Journaling:** Travelers can use CoPilot to document their travel experiences, capturing memories, recording observations, and organizing their travel plans.

- Project Documentation: Professionals can use CoPilot to document their projects, tracking progress, recording challenges, and reflecting on their accomplishments.

Examples of Using CoPilot as a Journal in Action

Here are some examples of how CoPilot might be used as a journal:

- A user uses CoPilot to document their daily experiences, reflecting on their interactions, challenges, and achievements. CoPilot analyzes their entries and provides a summary of their emotional state and recurring themes.

- A writer uses CoPilot to explore different writing styles and experiment with language. CoPilot provides feedback on their writing, suggests improvements, and helps them develop their creative voice.

- An individual in therapy uses CoPilot to document their therapy sessions, recording their thoughts, feelings, and progress. CoPilot helps them track their emotional well-being and identify areas for growth.

- A traveler uses CoPilot to document their travel experiences, capturing photos, recording audio notes, and creating a multimedia journal of their adventures.

Challenges and Considerations

While using CoPilot as a journal offers many benefits, there are also challenges and considerations:

- **Privacy and Security: Ensuring the privacy and security of personal journal entries is crucial. CoPilot needs to provide robust security measures to protect user data from unauthorized access.**

- **Data Ownership and Control: Users need to have control over their journal data, with the ability to export, edit, and delete their entries as needed.**

- **Emotional Sensitivity: CoPilot needs to be sensitive to the emotional content of journal entries, providing supportive and appropriate responses.**

- **Ethical Considerations: The use of AI in journaling raises ethical considerations, such as the potential for AI to misinterpret or misuse personal information.**

The Future of Journaling with AI

The future of journaling with AI is promising, with the potential to transform the way we document and reflect on our lives. As AI technology continues to advance, we can expect to see:

- **More Personalized Journaling Experiences:** AI will provide more personalized journaling experiences, tailoring prompts, feedback, and insights to individual user needs and preferences.

- **Integration with Mental Health Tools:** AI-powered journaling will be integrated with mental health tools, providing users with support, resources, and connections to mental health professionals.

- **AI-Driven Insights into Personal Growth:** AI will provide deeper and more insightful analysis of journal entries, helping users to gain a better understanding of their personal growth, identify areas for improvement, and achieve their goals.

- **New Forms of Journaling Expression:** AI will enable new forms of journaling expression, such as interactive journals, collaborative journals, and AI-generated creative content within journal entries.

Conclusion

Using CoPilot as a journal offers a powerful new way to document, reflect on, and gain insights from our personal experiences. By leveraging the capabilities of AI, CoPilot can enhance the journaling process, providing users with a more organized, insightful, and supportive platform for self-reflection and personal growth. As AI technology continues to evolve, the potential for CoPilot to transform the way we journal is limitless, paving the way for a future where AI empowers us to better understand ourselves and navigate our lives.

Chapter 18: CoPilot Integrated

The true power of CoPilot is realized when it's not just a standalone application, but rather a seamless and integrated part of our digital ecosystem. "CoPilot Integrated" represents this vision, exploring how CoPilot is woven into various platforms, applications, and services to enhance productivity, streamline workflows, and provide a more intuitive and unified user experience. This chapter delves into the concept of CoPilot integration, examining its different forms, benefits, and transformative impact on how we interact with technology.

Imagine CoPilot not as a separate entity, but as an invisible hand that assists you across your digital landscape, anticipating your needs, providing contextual support, and simplifying your tasks. That's the essence of CoPilot Integrated.

The Importance of AI Integration

AI integration is crucial for maximizing the effectiveness and usability of AI assistants. By embedding AI capabilities into the tools and platforms we use every day, we can:

- **Reduce Friction:** Integrate AI can reduce the friction of usIng AI, making it more accessible and convenient.

- **Enhance Productivity:** AI integration can enhance productivity by automating tasks, streamlining workflows, and providing contextual assistance.

- **Improve User Experience:** AI integration can improve the user experience by making technology more intuitive, responsive, and personalized.

- **Create Unified Workflows:** AI integration can create unified workflows, allowing users to perform tasks across different applications and platforms without switching between them.

CoPilot Integrated embodies this principle, aiming to bring the power of AI assistance to where users need it most, within the applications and services they rely on.

Forms of CoPilot Integration

CoPilot integration can take various forms, including:

- **Application Integration:** CoPilot can be integrated directly into applications, such as productivity suites, creative tools, and communication platforms.

- **Operating System Integration:** CoPilot can be integrated into the operating system, providing system-wide assistance and enhancing the user's overall computing experience.

- **Browser Integration:** CoPilot can be integrated into web browsers, providing AI assistance for web browsing, information retrieval, and online tasks.

- **Device Integration:** CoPilot can be integrated into various devices, such as smartphones, tablets, and smart devices, providing AI assistance across different platforms.

Benefits of CoPilot Integrated

CoPilot Integrated offers numerous benefits:

- **Increased Productivity: CoPilot can automate tasks, streamline workflows, and provide contextual assistance within the applications users are already using, boosting productivity.**

- **Enhanced Efficiency: By providing quick access to AI assistance and automating repetitive tasks, CoPilot can help users save time and effort.**

- **Improved User Experience: CoPilot integration makes technology more intuitive and user-friendly, providing a more seamless and natural way to interact with digital tools.**

- **Contextual Assistance: CoPilot can provide contextual assistance, understanding the user's current activity and providing relevant information and support.**

- **Unified Digital Experience: CoPilot integration creates a more unified digital experience, allowing users to perform tasks across different applications and platforms without switching between them.**

Examples of CoPilot Integration

Here are some examples of how CoPilot might be integrated:

- **CoPilot in Microsoft Office:** CoPilot is integrated into Microsoft Word, Excel, PowerPoint, and other Office applications, providing assistance with document creation, data analysis, and presentation design.

- **CoPilot in Windows:** CoPilot is integrated into the Windows operating system, providing system-wide assistance with tasks such as file management, settings adjustments, and application control.

- **CoPilot in Web Browsers:** CoPilot is integrated into web browsers, providing assistance with web browsing, information retrieval, and online tasks such as summarizing web pages and generating content.

- **CoPilot in Mobile Devices:** CoPilot is integrated into mobile operating systems and apps, providing AI assistance for tasks such as scheduling, communication, and navigation.

Challenges and Considerations

While CoPilot integration offers significant benefits, there are also challenges and considerations:

- Seamlessness of Integration: Ensuring a seamless and intuitive integration of CoPilot into different platforms and applications is crucial.

- Consistency of Experience: Providing a consistent and unified CoPilot experience across different integration points is important.

- Customization and Control: Users need to have control over CoPilot's integration, with the ability to customize settings and adjust its behavior.

- Privacy and Security: Protecting user privacy and ensuring data security is essential when integrating CoPilot into various applications and services.

The Future of AI Integration

The future of AI integration is promising, with AI assistants becoming increasingly embedded into our digital lives. We can expect to see:

- Deeper Integration: AI assistants will be more deeply integrated into our operating systems, applications, and devices, becoming an invisible and ubiquitous part of our digital experience.

- Proactive Assistance: AI assistants will become more proactive, anticipating our needs and providing timely assistance based on context and behavior.

- **Personalized AI Experiences:** AI integration will enable more personalized AI experiences, tailoring assistance and recommendations to individual user preferences.

- **AI-Powered Ecosystems:** AI integration will lead to the development of AI-powered ecosystems, where different applications and services work together seamlessly, enhancing productivity and efficiency.

Conclusion

CoPilot Integrated represents a crucial step in the evolution of AI assistants, moving beyond standalone applications to a more unified and seamless digital experience. By embedding CoPilot into the tools and platforms we use every day, we can unlock the full potential of AI assistance, enhancing productivity, improving user experience, and transforming the way we interact with technology. As AI integration continues to advance, we can expect to see a future where AI assistants become an indispensable part of our digital lives, empowering us to achieve more and navigate the digital world with greater ease and efficiency.

Learn by Using CoPilot

Lesson 1: Getting Started with CoPilot

- Objective: Introduce readers to the basics of CoPilot.

- Assignment:

    - Install CoPilot on your device (desktop or mobile).

    - Use CoPilot to perform a simple task, such as summarizing a document or generating a list of ideas for a project.

    - Reflect on how CoPilot's suggestions align with your expectations.

Lesson 2: CoPilot in Word

- Objective: Teach readers how to use CoPilot for document creation.

- Assignment:

    - Open a blank Word document and ask CoPilot to generate an outline for a report on a topic of your choice.

    - Use CoPilot to rewrite a paragraph in a more professional tone.

- o Create a table of contents using CoPilot's formatting tools.

Lesson 3: CoPilot for Research

- Objective: Show readers how to use CoPilot for deep research.
- Assignment:
    - o Ask CoPilot to summarize a complex article or research paper.
    - o Request citations for the information provided by CoPilot.
    - o Compare CoPilot's research capabilities with traditional search engines.

Lesson 4: CoPilot for Creative Tasks

- Objective: Explore CoPilot's creative capabilities.
- Assignment:
    - o Use CoPilot to generate a short story or poem based on a prompt.
    - o Ask CoPilot to create an image based on a description.

- Reflect on how CoPilot's creativity compares to human creativity.

Lesson 5: CoPilot Integration

- Objective: Demonstrate how CoPilot integrates with other tools.

- Assignment:

  - Use CoPilot to schedule a meeting in Outlook.

  - Ask CoPilot to summarize an email thread.

  - Use CoPilot to control a smart home device (if applicable).